Long Day in Rehab

Joshua R. Leuthold

Long Day in Rehab
Copyright © 2013 Joshua R. Leuthold

Published by Green Hill Press
South Bend, IN

ISBN-10: 0-9911319-3-2
ISBN-13: 978-0-9911319-3-8

Book & cover design: Joshua R. Leuthold
Cover image: Cassandra Leuthold

For Kathy & all you've done for me over the years. Sorry it took so long for you to get to read some of my poetry.

& Cassandra for your love, your support, & your help reigniting the passion for words within me.

Table of Contents

Cre(m)ation

Soft piano music fills my head with blue & I sit here putting black
on white, ash on slate(once done in caves, on walls, with blood
of berries, now done in abstract, using ones & zeros in a formless
fiber optic maze, wary of the minotaur, saving early & often, entropy
given imagined space to dwell inside plastic & silicon boxes, lit up
by liquid crystals & plasma, the smell of hot metal fills
the room & mingles with the scent of coffee or tea or incense
or light fixtures left on too long, & my fingers bleed like berries
from the childbirth/abortion/menstruation/stillbirth of ideas,
& if I had a funeral for every time I lost one of my children
I'd never leave the cemetery).

Sometimes you choose to light the fire, other times the flame
reaches for you. Contractions tighten & cramp places you didn't know
existed, then you find yourself stranded in the dark with nothing
but a computer monitor to light your way out(or through to the other side
of the void/vacuum/hell/hole/door where you see the forms take shape
into shadows & breathless gasps of light pollution against a backdrop
of smoke&mirror bravery left in piecemeal fallacies & testy lines
of textual brilliance – electricity scarring the silent tornado imprint with...)

The Tumble(r) took the (story)Teller by the throat, threw (him) up
(in)to the (ceiling) fan, & watched him as he (got) (kid)napped.
Now penetrating those rose bushes kept pristine
by gunslingers & malcontents with their bloodshot eyes & handlebar mustaches,
shooting seed(s) all over the fertile earth(grinning with well-intentioned malice,
teeth shining like knife-blades in the black-light darkness of...)

As the dust settles a match is struck on a thumb gone rough
with typing/writing/erasing/revising & holding that (nose to the grinds)tone.
Magnesium flare set against a backdrop of cerulean crescendo(strings
charged with bolts of soft lightning, hold the thunder, that comes
later & beats a(n) (ear)drum in the eye of the (brain)storm) catches
the gas nozzle just right & solidifies the work like fine
masonry(meant to last/endure/weather/withstand & leave
a monument to make a statement) taking the granite for granted
as a reality built then bent before breaking to burnt embers.

Keep the spent cinders of cremation handy, you never know
when you'll need more ink or paint or lead or clay or canvas
or cellulose or silicon or the ashes of forgotten fragments
& abandoned creations...

Automatic Writhing

They were eyes in a skull like pennies
air has oxidized. Dreams of green & gold over heads with hair
of a similar color. Given options of rust or ruin left little choice
to make, molecules drift, the way wind & water are atoms
punching us in the face.

I heard I was too far out

& a void opened up to swallow piano music into inhaled smoke,
taste of dead channel static on cotton tongue, the way the holy loses
luster when idols tarnish, & purity of stillness, clarity

of a body not in motion

given to saline thoughts:

  driftwood, soap, old buckets filled with paint,
  blood, & another droplet falls silent...

I felt a splinter before I saw a squirrel run along a fence,
fur-covered body suspended in sunshine with a seed held close
& there's material here for another scene, something private poured
over hot coals, steam collected, pumped through séance
into distilled illusion & pondered

by glassy-eyed ghouls gasping disapproval at double-meanings.

Falling Asleep While Watching a Television Tuned to Dead Channel Noise

What is there left

behind

when dreams have evaporated:

porous thoughts

faded

like so much vapor, steam

of consciousness leaving

condensation

drips

on paper

Engaged in this High Definition

dissertation

I find I can't find

memories

to develop meaning
from nothing.

Balance
A Tribute to Coil.

There's an irony in ashes, soiled sheets offer up a linen caress
& like silk we struggle:

> threaded through flaps of flesh
> suturing the screaming mouth shut.

Turn shit into gold,
scattered through our brains:

> wings flutter a liminal hymn
> with a resonance to rub against
> my unquiet skull...

Left aghast this gash:

> watching the snow you've captured rapture,
> ruptured bone with vodka tumble, & seen on the scene
> locks of golden hair & a voice of silver, slivered
> into strands like threadbare rugs dusted in gray
> & thrown to dumpsters

Fall, so frail, against broken windowpanes, shards of glass
slash fragile wrists. Silver slivers pierce the boat's bottom
as it slides down the tunnel. Wallow away from the hollow
not knowing what slipped inside.

Haunted by paranoid inlay, fear set inside our aside, from notes
given in chaos, scattered brain redirects energy of orgasm
until the organism is fresh, less fragile, empty & spent.

This weight, bare but glinting in halogen light-flare, beneath a cloud
where the dead are left alone with a nimbus of intensity. One way
transmission (melancholy, echoing across dead testaments,
empty tenements, false atonements), statements vacant as cracked porcelain.

A glitch in darkened rooms plays with ironies, chaos, compound accidents,
& death meant to mean we're making meanings, crackling static
of a lonely microphone in an abandoned room, through the ear canal, a tremble

from the ambience, scramble above, tasting forever the noise as the ambulance died with siren sounds...

Hush.

Washing Dirt from a Forgotten Chalk Tiger

1.

"You left some art here," his voice splinters into electricity, running
through cords to her ear.

"Do whatever with it," her voice clipping with echoes from hanging up.

> *Where is she?*

Mind adrift, he stares at the ceiling fan, blades whirling
forever, rotations pointless as orbiting space junk.

They are all here:

> *Pocket watch.*
> *Oil lamps.*
> *Notes she wrote*
> *& Unfinished Paper Tiger (staring at him with half-face,*
> *she said it was crap, & he told her to finish it, because it was beautiful,*
> *& still is:*
>
>> sitting in solitude on his porch, cold in January, hot in July,
>> paper turning yellow while the tiger blurs & melts from changes
>> in moisture—temperature(the press of fingers)...)

2.

He frames thoughts with a head full of ink & static,
palm sweat sticks in the grooves of his hands & the smell of rubber cement
fills his nose:

> *I shouldn't have formed half-fists to carve letters from white-noise of paper.*

Stuck in awkward poses with books he'll never read, a throw-away futon
that won't fit in the moving van, some pots & pans, a queen-sized bed,
& a knife set (wooden handles worn, shine removed by time, patina of blades dulled
by use, not meant to be left behind...).

3.

When we spoke of weather I knew he'd forgotten:

> *Smell of fresh air through hotel window, combination coffee & exhaust,*
> *left holding a cigarette & pretending not to care...*

"What happened to dreams?" his voice breaking against waves—pulsing tone of the disconnected phone.

Some Strange Sadness

A sound board for suffering in silence, something less
than brief (the way bruises heal yellow) & there was that space
we filled with laughter.

Still, we never said what was or should have been spoken:

> *light shines in flickering waves, heat on flesh & cold of shadows. Scratching*
> *surface textures with a seam ripper (dreams fading in a steady dissolve*
> *to sunrise, smiles, & slips of the tongue).*

Wanting sex with strippers but settling for the soft
release of loneliness & pornography. Drinking in sadness
from a lead-lined cup, watching & waiting for a refill,
for some sign of the waitress & her endless carafe (creamer,
sugar, & black fades to soft brown-yellow,
colors of escape, of wicked ways easily forgotten).

Riding until out of fuel & stumbling into an awkward
morning of lost clothes, hangover, & nameless goodbye,
sun staining the sky with rust & nicotine, a busted tape
deck playing backwards & forwards in an endless loop,
a dream left unbroken (like a time before this
all began – warm, dark, & full of hope).

Hope

I gave up once:

> *purple clouds laced overhead like crooked fingers,*
> *left to follow empty spaces into dripping consciousness*
> *of spent yearnings, so much green & yellow, the kind*
> *that blurs the lines & gives pause before movement,*
> *torrent, a surge of wind & rain into a sort of scorn,*
> *trees bent sideways, reaching over to grab one-another,*
> *splintered cracks rain down in wooden cascade...*

There was a twisting sensation & the spirals I drew on paper
were left alone to wrinkle with time & salt water drops,
fighting against exhaustion & failing.

Eyes floating in coffee,
lurking above a bleeding pen.

Two hands draw one-another in a warped world
of plastic & flash paper, drop a match into water & let the whisper
die; sizzle giving breath to beaten paths in brain wrinkles.

Watch single heartbeats across a line become music heard through
vacant rooms, shadow-play transforming silhouettes into sharp objects.

I left the window open & felt a breeze tear away at an empty page
before I stood below the half moon & set fire to a stolen car.

A.Hol(e): ^{above}AND$_{below}$

Look ^{up} and look out$_{(side\ yourself)}$
at a d^{i}st$_o$rt^i_on of perceptions (preceptions/prescriptions/
                                    deceptions/conceptions/
                                    conceived/conceit/concentration/
                                    meditation/dissipation/
                                    transubstantiation)
and you're left doing that $^{high\text{-}horse}$ act of attrition,
or is it in addi|c|tion to a diction?
Sal|i|vation comin' to a l

                    e

              f

        t

                  -handed tetragrammaton (tetrahedron/tesseract/
                                        teleology/topology)
    looking $_{down}$ to-ward (off) spirits
    i'mb|r|ibed to |s|wallow (in) this self-pi|e|ty
    on my knees again and spi$_{lling}$ sli d i n g__(o u   t)
grindingagain|st|($_{bone}$AND^{sinew}AND$_{fragmentary\ grenades}$ thrown at the sun)
this |atro|city wetting my dryeyes with saline and blisters
how can I do anything but dr|ip|ink (or genuflect)?

See or beseen in this scene of screams and silver screens,
or watch|mak(ers)|ing as you dwindle $_{down}$ to-ward (off) nothing|ness|
Your haloes and silver bullets left to dr i f t
until **-cancelled-** at which time you're left with **-blank-**
taste|s|-bud|s| and cigarette|s| burn|s|
dismayed(decayed/delayed/denied/defied/desecrated)
with a con(ju|gal|[ror's]) touch,
    and score|d| with a pen(|is|cil) and a minimalist (|h|ear) for|e(skin)ground| sound
      these shiFtIN$_g$ images (of/a)bound(less ingenuity)

Singing:
        Alcohol and cinema sittin' in a tree,
        ess-you-see-kay-eye-en-jee
        one going in, the other flopping down,
        which one more likely to make you frown?

Finally–
Smell the broken wind and greasy food of the bar and grin,
discourse consists of back-patting and ego-stroking until
left alone to dine on misery and the black below,
you order again and then go home,
falling asleep to Lynch-ings and the sound of Finche|r|s
and nightmaring about the return of Prohibition.

Wandering a Modern Maze

1.

City night fluorescent
as a public restroom:

> *dirt climbs the cracks*
> *between tiles, faucets tarnished*
> *by filthy fingers(mirror-smudged*
> *faces become ghosts staring*
> *from brush strokes)*

He sees his reflection
in pedestrian faces, eyes
glinting like sewer water.

Wanders past a fruit stand,
tangerines exhausted as tailpipes,
the citrus & gasoline smell
of homemade napalm,
an el train roars
with its electric & mechanical voice
singing a scraping steel song;
a minotaur in this modern maze.

Fists come out of cars to beat him,
a kick in the ribs & his eyes
flutter against grit-covered concrete.

He looks up & sees
a wounded dumpster, bleeding
rust from a laceration.

2.

A voice comes at me sideways
from an alley & the bricks peel
back to show their fangs.

My tie whips:

> *breeze stirs pressed fabric*
> *against impossible*
> *streetlight (beneath windows*
> *watching from above)*

The drawn quality of city life:

> *taxi cabs as tiny universes*
> *inside yellow scabs, the landscape*
> *breathes steam at 3am, & I'm trapped*
> *inside angry walls.*

3.

He sees chewing gum on cement
when he steps on the street

into open space.

Black & round,
a beauty mark,
a mole,
& he thinks about people
living beneath the city:

> *flashes of light*
> *cast shadows in empty tunnels,*
> *more dust than he'll ever breathe, layers*
> *of soft silt cover forgotten pathways of convenience,*
> *& tile mosaics wink whenever a fire is used*
> *to cook a rat.*

The way soot gathers over head,
sounds of distant trains
rumble, & buildings stare down at him,
derelict bricks leering like broken teeth as he walks
through the streets.

Home is a tower crying alone against the sky,
cut into clouds, & he's asking if lightning

rods scrape holes in the ozone.

4.

For the fifth time in two weeks
a series of squares have been drawn
on smooth black skin.

Those pink temporary tattoos
wash off in the rain, but dignity
heals scarred as oil stains…

Little girls play hopscotch, sweating
beneath the sun.

They'll be gone soon, either dead or
escaped or moved on to new neighborhoods.
Faces will change—though
the game stays—& gouged
out bits of concrete, crags on a weathered face,
will always remember most fondly

feet that stepped instead of hopped.

Acid Rain Etches Tears on Lonely Brick

The girl on the street was aware of the texture
he presented, but said little with her flat affect.

Left to scrape by on cans & bottles he pulled
a wallet out of the air then circled the room
looking for something white to bleed on. The hawk
left to fly in an empty field—racing against the giant clock
of nocturnal living. This mindless meandering
of individuals in the acid rain—melodramas
& fake lives lived behind broken-glass masks,
mosaic replicas mass-produced in a tile factory then sold
at gouged rates to idiot tourists.

These are the dumpsters he loves, carved into the alley,
& left alone—the sound of solid sand breaking
like a vase of white roses dropped on a kitchen floor,
abandoned & withering in the pale light of dusk.

He sighed, smiled in satisfaction at the tinkle
of shards, so many rain drops on rooftop tin, then left her
to watch helplessly as he drained a blister on her
torn-up bed.

Imprints

It's when lightning
streaks across a velvet
breach in the sky &
strikes my cranial nerves
that electricity
gets channeled through my
fingertips:

> *Paint in the purple &*
> *crimson rust-colored*
> *sunset—birds chirp in bushes*
> *then fly away, wings*
> *beat hard against black up-*
> *drafts, the temperature of cooling*
> *lava, exposed oils & cadmium,*
> *carbon colors on acid-free paper*

It's when I bite
my tongue that I taste
the world:

> *metallic, salty*
> *with a hint of garlic,*
> *like blood climbing cracks*
>
> *between teeth*

that everything clinks together
in the frame of my vision:

> *ice in the bottom of a brandy snifter,*
>
> *the sound more whisper than laugh*

From Here to Chicago

1.

There are days it burns
like asphalt, beach sand,
or the sun-scorched skin
that peeled in the shower
after our day together

that summer, I remember:

> *aloe*
> *& your fingertips*
>
> *as they brushed flesh.*
>
> *I shuddered against the sting,*
> *your touch, & apologies*
> *when my breath hissed*
> *from my lips.*

Something stirs inside,
wanting out, walking sideways
like a crab, or children playing

a strange game.

2.

Distance:

> *mileage & gallons of gasoline*
> *send waves of vapor*
>
> *through the air.*

While we were home
the numbers grew

from here

to Chicago

infill housing

chokes empty space.

Blankets

There was a blanket pulled over
sunrise; a wrapping-paper-pink day crumbled
& thrown out

lands gasping in the breeze against a bent curb
undulations match the flicker of dancing flame
until I came along & saw:

>　　*agonal breathing*
>　　*shallow pulse*
>　　*cold extremities*

Swept into arms, kissed lips to tissue
& brought the light back

But beneath the blanks it fell

like ash or snow gone gray from tires travelling
away & dropped to the dirt

wet like clay, left in gutters by rain water

never again lit by flame.

Somewhere in the Middle of All That Noise

Broken clouds bleed faded sunshine,
light diffused into fragments, the gray of dead television,
& we ran through puddles formed before morning.

Freedom mixed with fear & the failures of friends,
sitting now, on a river's rocky shoreline, listening to lisps
of busted engines from the hill above,

those empty things (dreams).

What was left to ponder became memories,

shrapnel & stories about death & time spent
inside the abandoned mental hospital

spray paint leaving lasting impressions in neon

& I left because of a cold spot

& a whisper in the rec room.

Red: Cloud Cover Echoed on Bleached Bones

Stillness is the point but I'm still in the waveform
& the sound we don't see, fires blooming in rock formations
sent across fields of sagebrush on beams of sunlight.

Glare echoes in my eyes, vision cloudy with clear blue sky
& each step takes me further out, into waves sending ripples
across empty space, a crunching beneath feet & bleached
bones watching with motionless sockets.

Sometimes red comes out & we smear it along the ridges,
coloring minerals crimson, looking for water until dusk
causes quiet & our tracks lie undisturbed beneath an unbroken skyline.

We came back together in the end, along the flow of a vacant road
where the only object dividing dying light was our transportation.

Somewhere Between Illinois & Ohio the Painting Ceased

1.

This is meditation:

> *throat scratchy from screaming or weather change*
> *lines forming beneath white of fog & still air,*
> *stubbed out cigarettes in dashboard ashtrays,*
> *hash marks white in dying daylight & passing*
> *between, cracks in asphalt, a single pool of water*
> *giving birth to a single green sprout...*

Gross vanity of horsepower:

> *engine roar punctuates movement,*
> *grasping at catching slow fade of red & gold*
> *& orange-turning-blue-becoming-purple. Centered*
> *by pressure on the pedal, eased into speed meant*
> *solely for self or to run away from something else,*
> *metal given meaning, rainfall twists fluorescence*
> *into abstract feelings, painting emotions in bent light...*

2.

We touched on emptiness one gallon at a time
bathed as we were in the bright white beams of gas
station lights, she asked me for a cigarette & I felt
a fire start without my lighter.

3.

I found focus once:

> *arms draped over the wheel, a dead stop at a red light*
> *sent waves of frustration flowing into an impatient foot,*
> *crunch of steel against steel, bumpers bent, & we met*
> *in anger; later: dinner & laughter then passion & pleasure,*
> *but first hypertensive with nervous tension, nostrils flared*
> *from forced breathing, & eyes shone like meteors flown*
> *through blue skies, moments meant to merge lives in obvious directions...*

4.

...painted lines pressed against vision until
the brush stopped mid stroke.

Amphetamines as Gasoline

Take two small red pills:

> *wind whips snow tendrils across the road*
> *like ash after a bonfire started in dry leaves left*
> *alone & given space to be blown through darkness*
> *with little more shining down than a crescent moon*

& give them half an hour to work...

30 minutes later, a wave like summer
washes over, & deletes the gray filter.

Remember Empty Rooms with Dust & Smoke

1.

A mirror-life left listless

snaps into place.

The problem is:

> *everyone paints in reflections.*

I recall the clothes you sewed & my fear of judgment.

Wanted to buy a new canvas
in vulgar fashion,

instead bought a new bucket of paint.

Then:

> *dented in a corner,*
> *rusted skin covered with age spots,*
> *gathered dust forming fine hairs...*

Tripped over the withered cord
that held us in place:

> *fell down & resisted pressure, antisocial,*
> *dissociative —words meant to burn, sparked*
> *the smell of aluminum cans in a bonfire.*

A transition as thick as smoke of melted
Styrofoam:

> *when you leave the world behind*
> *& strike off on your own path*
> *carved through beaten trees*
> *with a rib machete, crawl*
> *on the ground like a fresh amputee,*
> *stumps still bleed sap,*
> *or perhaps...*

2.

He left oxford collars stained the brown of dried blood
& I saw him:

> *alone with self-indulgence,*
> *adrift & peaceful in the lake of names—asking himself:*
>
> is there ever enough?

Multiple Myeloma & Small Cell Carcinoma

1.

She sits cross-legged
on the floor
folding laundry with him
watching her from the comfort
of the couch.

She can see him
trying to remember:

> The physician found
> the hematological malignancy
> after the phlebotomist drew
> serum into a syringe containing
> an anticoagulant.
> "This is to keep the specimen from
> hemolyzing," the phlebotomist
> told them.
> Followed by:
>> peripheral blood smears, cytogenetics
>> (including fluorescent *in situ* hybridization,
>> or FISH, he had joked with her
>> that the physician was just going FISHing,
>> & her laugh sounded like a tree exhaling
>> after being struck with an axe).
>> Immunophenotyping came next. Afterward
>> the physician said the test was inconclusive
>> but pointed to multiple myeloma.
>>> Confirmation

>>>> required a bone marrow biopsy.

∎ ∎ ∎

The velour sweater is soft
between her fingertips as she bends

cloth & folds it
into the plastic hamper.
A skeleton sitting still,
fresh putty smeared
over brittle bones, & staring
through her cancelled eyes
seeing the way he supports
a bowing structure.
She's trying
to remember:

> Sharp pain from bone marrow aspiration
> followed by acute turmoil. "What
> are my options?"

> The physician laid out treatments:
>> relief of symptoms using common induction regimes
>> such as *VAD*, melphalan, & dexamethasone with thalidomide.
>> If the symptoms stabilize aggressive chemotherapy
>> & hematopoietic stem cell transplantation.

2.

The cancer was a hammer
that hit him hard
in the chest,
& he had to be
an anvil.

As time went by options dwindled:
> Vincristine, Adriamycin, melphalan, & dexamethasone
> did nothing.
> Cachectic, she became a skeleton unable to eat,
> & often pointing at her central line, calling it her Space Communicator,
> smiling her empty-humored smile, teeth like bone-shards grown
> from the garden of her gums.

■ ■ ■

Starting at age 12:

> A pack of smokes a day
> in back of the hardware store,
> a pressure in his mind
> from the teasing of his cousin,
> despite the warnings on those labels,
> tried to quit twice before,
> now reliant on the relief of an occasional five minute break
> from life.

He remembers her:
> soft touch when his back was sore,
> the way her hands
> were always cold
> beneath the covers,
> soothing his hot flesh,
> & that day
> when it was just
> her & him
> in the movie theater to see
> the film about
> a man,
> a woman,
> & a missed opportunity.
> The way they'd held each other in the dark,
> her tears wetting his shoulder
> through a button-up shirt.
> His struggle to remain tearless
> an attempt to comfort with stability.

3.

He hacks to get breath,
crimson tissues scattered across his chest,
dead soldiers lost on the plaid field
of his woolen shirt, blood clots on their white uniforms.

He remembers in a wave like liquid
asphalt, tar-black & covering him
in webs of tobacco juice:

> Having filled a box of Puffs
> with blood, he went to the doctor.
> Two chest x-rays & a computed
> axial tomography scan later the physician
> said that the hemoptysis was from bronchi
> irritation due to the heavy coughing, &
> the coughing was caused by (the doctor paused
> here, & that's how he knew it was bad news,
> they never come in somber if it's good news,
> he learned that much) small cell lung
> carcinoma. "What are my options?" The question
> burning gray in the air.
> "I'm afraid there are none, it's already metastasized—"
>
> "Metastasized – I've heard that before, so it's spread?"
>
> "Yes, to your brain, heart, liver, & spine.
> You only have a month left."
>
> "But my wife…"
>
> "I'm sorry."

4.

She looks up at the yellowed wall,
pictures hanging like memorials
to the missing.

The way they were together hanging over
the way they are now in ashen clouds
of vanishing life.

She stands, knees popping,
& grabs the photograph of him fishing

on the lake in the spring,
morning light filters through the lens
of the camera in a golden glare,
white cigarette obscuring his smile.

Her vision blurs & steams,
drops like contrast on a slide
smear the color of his red fishing
jacket into ruby gobs that glisten
in the sheen of fresh blood.

She looks back to him, his hands & feet cyanotic blue & white,
the dyspnea forcing him to gasp for breath, his bones barely binding
together beneath the taught fabric of his flesh as he reaches up to wipe
his mouth, the tissue pulling back crimson-on-white,
hands shuddering with pain.

5.

He looks at her pillowy personality, everything
about her warm; a blanket of compassion, gazes
into her eyes & tries to tell her something, but
only creaks like a door with rusty hinges.

About the Author

Joshua Leuthold is a rehabilitated writer. After years of wordsmith neglect, he has been repaired by his wife, Cassandra, who has always remained a writer, uninterrupted. He lives in a house much larger than his small two person & a cat family requires. Enjoying the finer things in life: well-written books, homemade meals, a good cup of coffee, great films, television, tabletop role-playing games, & video games, it's amazing he gets any writing done at all.